Fighting Dinosaurs
by Monica Hughes

Consultant: Luis M. Chiappe, Ph.D.
Director of the Dinosaur Institute
Natural History Museum of Los Angeles County

BEARPORT
PUBLISHING

NEW YORK, NEW YORK

Credits

Cover, Title Page, 4, 5, 10–11, 18, 20, 22B: Luis Rey; 6: John Alston; 8–9, 12, 15, 21, 22T: Natural History Museum; 13, 16–17, 23: Lisa Alderson; 17, 19: © Simon Mendez; 7: Bob Nicholls; 14: Ian Jackson.

Every effort has been made by ticktock Entertainment Ltd. to trace copyright holders. We apologize in advance for any omissions. We would be pleased to insert the appropriate acknowledgments in any subsequent edition of this publication.

Library of Congress Cataloging-in-Publication Data

Hughes, Monica.
  Fighting dinosaurs / by Monica Hughes.
    p. cm. — (I love reading. Dino world!)
  Includes bibliographical references and index.
  ISBN-13: 978-1-59716-545-7 (library binding)
  ISBN-10: 1-59716-545-X (library binding)
  1. Dinosaurs—Juvenile literature. I. Title.

QE861.5.H84 2008
567.9—dc22

                            2007017960

For more information, write to Bearport Publishing Company, Inc., 101 Fifth Avenue, Suite 6R, New York, New York 10003. Printed in the United States of America.

10 9 8 7 6 5 4 3 2 1

Contents

Built to fight

Many dinosaurs had bodies made for fighting.

Some dinosaurs fought with their hard heads.

Stygimoloch
(stij-ee-MOLL-ok)

Other dinosaurs used their sharp **claws** in battle.

Segnosaurus
(*seg*-noh-SOR-uhss)

5

Why did dinosaurs fight?

Meat-eating dinosaurs ate other dinosaurs.

So they often had to fight to kill their food.

Albertosaurus
(al-*bur*-toh-SOR-uhss)

They used their sharp teeth and strong jaws.

Tyrannosaurus rex
(ti-*ran*-uh-SOR-uhss REKS)

A big meat-eater

Allosaurus was one of the biggest meat-eating dinosaurs.

It had long claws and about 70 pointed teeth.

It killed plant-eating dinosaurs, like *Dryosaurus*.

Dryosaurus
(**drye**-oh-**SOR**-uhss)

Allosaurus
(*al*-oh-SOR-uhss)

9

Small killer dinosaurs

Not all meat-eating dinosaurs were big.

Deinonychus was a small dinosaur.

Several of them sometimes fought as a group.

Deinonychus
(dye-NON-ih-kuhss)

10

Together, they could kill bigger dinosaurs.

Plant-eaters

Most dinosaurs ate only plants.

Some of these dinosaurs were very big.

Their huge size helped scare off dinosaurs that wanted to fight.

Seismosaurus is one of the longest animals that ever lived.

It was up to 130 feet (40 m) long!

Seismosaurus
(*size*-moh-SOR-uhss)

Brachiosaurus is one of the tallest animals found so far.

It could grow up to 50 feet (15 m) tall!

**Brachiosaurus
(brak-ee-oh-SOR-uhss)**

Fast and scary

Some plant-eaters were fast.

Hypsilophodon could run away
from fights.

Hypsilophodon
(hip-sih-LOH-fuh-don)

Other plant-eaters, like *Styracosaurus*, looked scary.

Meat-eating dinosaurs ran away from them.

On its nose, *Styracosaurus* had a horn as long as a sword.

Styracosaurus
(sti-*rak*-oh-SOR-uhss)

Horns and spines

Some plant-eating dinosaurs had to fight meat-eaters.

Some had horns or **spines** to protect themselves.

Sauropelta had spines on its neck.

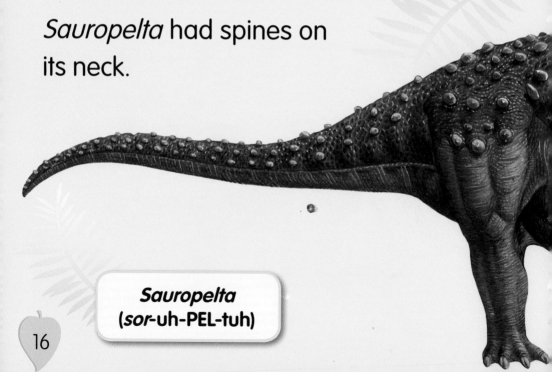

Sauropelta
(*sor*-uh-PEL-tuh)

Triceratops had three horns on its head.

17

Plates

Some plant-eaters had hard **plates** on their bodies.

The plates protected them in fights.

Scutellosaurus had small plates covering its back and tail.

Scutellosaurus
(skoo-*tel*-oh-SOR-uhss)

Stegosaurus had two rows of plates on its back.

It also had spines at the end of its tail.

Stegosaurus
(*steg*-uh-**SOR-uhss**)

Armor and clubs

Tarchia had **armor** to protect its body.

It also had a club at the end of its tail.

During a fight, it could hit meat-eating dinosaurs with the club.

Tarchia
(TAHR-kee-uh)

Euoplocephalus had armor and a tail club, too.

tail club

Euoplocephalus
(*yoo*-op-luh-SEF-uh-luhss)

Glossary

armor (AR-mur)
special bones that
protected dinosaurs

claws (KLAWZ)
sharp nails at
the end of the
fingers or toes
of an animal

plates (PLAYTS)
flat pieces of bone

spines (SPYNZ)
thin, pointy bones

23

Index

Read More

Dixon, Dougal. *Dinosaurs.* Honesdale, PA: Boyds Mill Press, Inc. (1998).

Malam, John, and Steve Parker. *Encyclopedia of Dinosaurs and Other Prehistoric Creatures.* New York: Barnes & Noble Books (2003).

Learn More Online

To learn more about the world of dinosaurs, visit

www.bearportpublishing.com/ILoveReading